# THE MAGNIFICENT BOOK

## BOOK

## ❖ OF ❖

## OCEAN CREATURES

# THE MAGNIFICENT BOOK

## OF

## OCEAN CREATURES

ILLUSTRATED BY

Val Walerczuk

WRITTEN BY

Tom Jackson

Silver Dolphin

Silver Dolphin Books
An imprint of Printers Row Publishing Group
A division of Readerlink Distribution Services, LLC
9717 Pacific Heights Blvd, San Diego, CA 92121
www.silverdolphinbooks.com

Printers Row Publishing Group is a division of Readerlink Distribution
Services, LLC.
Silver Dolphin Books is a registered trademark of Readerlink
Distribution Services, LLC.

All notations of errors or omissions should be addressed to Silver
Dolphin Books, Editorial Department, at the above address. All other
correspondence (author inquiries, permissions) concerning the
content of this book should be addressed to:
Weldon Owen Children's Books
An imprint of Weldon Owen International, L.P.
A subsidiary of Insight International, L.P.
PO Box 3088
San Rafael, CA 94912
www.insighteditions.com

ISBN: 978-1-64517-101-0
Manufactured, printed, and assembled in Humen, China.
Second printing, August 2022. RRD/08/22
26 25 24 23 22   2 3 4 5 6

# Introduction

From colorful coral reefs to the deep, dark sea, the world's oceans are teeming with creatures of all shapes, sizes, and colors. Whether it's the blue whale (the largest animal that has ever lived on Earth) or the many-legged sea star, our oceans are home to some of the most diverse life on the planet.

Each page of *The Magnificent Book of Ocean Creatures* showcases an animal with stunning, detailed illustrations paired with basic stats and fascinating facts. Inside, you'll find creatures that soar above the water, hide in the nooks and crannies of coral reefs, and make their homes atop chilly ice floes. Discover where each animal lives, what it eats, and how big it is compared to a 6-foot-tall human.

Which animal's name means "horse whale?" Whose tongue is as heavy as an elephant? Which creature's eyes are located on its arms? Find out these answers and many more as you dive in and discover all of the magnificent life in and around the ocean.

## Fact file

**Lives:** Worldwide

**Habitat:** Oceans

**Length:** 18 feet

**Weight:** 5,000 pounds

**Life span:** 70 years

**Diet:** Fish, seals, birds, and small whales

# Contents

# Sea otter

- A sea otter sleeps in the water while floating on its back.

- The otter eats shellfish. It cracks open the shells by hammering them with a flat stone. It also eats sea urchins.

- The otter stores its hammer stone in a loose pouch of skin on its chest.

- In rough waves, otters wrap seaweed around their bodies so they do not drift away.

- Sea otter fur is the thickest in the animal kingdom. A square inch of skin can have up to a million hairs growing out of it.

- Sea otters will sometimes link arms to form a "raft" so they can stay together as they float at the surface.

- Air bubbles trapped in the otter's thick fur keep it warm and enable it to float easily.

## Fact file

**Lives:** North Pacific Ocean
**Habitat:** Seaweed forests
**Length:** 4.5 feet
**Weight:** 70 pounds
**Life span:** 15 years
**Diet:** Shellfish and sea urchins

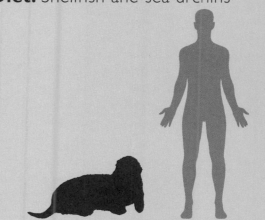

# Walrus

- Walruses can use their tusks to pull themselves out of the water onto floating ice.

- A walrus can hold its breath underwater for up to ten minutes.

- The walrus uses a sensitive moustache of bristles on its snout to feel for shellfish on the sandy seabed.

- When it finds some food, the walrus clears away the sand around it with a blast of air from its mouth.

- The tusks are the walrus's upper teeth. They can be more than three feet long.

Walruses fight by jabbing each other with their tusks. Their skin is nearly four inches thick, so the tusks do not do much damage.

A layer of fat, or blubber, underneath a walrus's skin keeps it warm. In winter, the walrus's body is one-third blubber!

## Fact file

**Lives:** Arctic Ocean

**Habitat:** Sea ice and beaches

**Length:** 10 feet

**Weight:** 2,200 pounds

**Life span:** 30 years

**Diet:** Clams and crustaceans

11

# Hooded seal

- Male hooded seals have a stretchy air bag, or hood, on their heads. When inflated, these hoods can be used to make loud calls.

- Male seals also show off their stretched hoods to attract a mate. Females prefer males with the brightest red bags.

- Female hooded seals give birth to babies on floating ice.

- A baby hooded seal, or pup, is fed milk by its mother for just four days. In that time the pup doubles in size.

- Hooded seal pups have white bellies and blue-gray backs, which helps them to hide among the ice floes.

- Hooded seals can dive more than 3,000 feet and stay underwater for nearly an hour at a time.

- These seals spend about 20 hours underwater every day.

## Fact file

**Lives:** North Atlantic and Arctic Oceans

**Habitat:** Ocean and pack ice

**Length:** 6–8.5 feet

**Weight:** 350–900 pounds

**Life span:** 35 years

**Diet:** Fish, crustaceans, krill, and squid

# Blue whale

- The blue whale is the largest animal known to have existed.

- A blue whale can eat up to 8,000 pounds of food in a single day.

- The whale's heart can weigh as much as a small car.

- A blue whale's call is so loud that it can be heard through the ocean more than 1,000 miles away.

- As the whale breathes out, it blows a spout of water 30 feet into the air.

- A newborn blue whale weighs nearly 6,000 pounds.

- Baby blue whales feed on their mother's milk and gain about 200 pounds per day in their first year of life.

## Fact file

**Lives:** Worldwide

**Habitat:** Deep ocean

**Length:** 80–100 feet

**Weight:** 400,000 pounds

**Life span:** 80 years

**Diet:** Krill

# Humpback whale

- Humpbacks are named for the long, low fin on their backs, which pokes out of the water when they swim.

- Humpbacks can spot ships and boats by poking their heads out of the water.

- The whale slaps its tail on the surface to make a loud noise. Scientists think that this behavior is a form of communication among whales.

- Humpbacks blow a wall of bubbles around schools of fish to keep them from swimming away—then the whales eat thousands of fish in one gulp!

- Each group, or pod, of humpback whales has a single song that members call to each other.

- Female humpbacks are a little larger than males.

- To jump completely out of the water, a humpback whale swims to the surface at 18 mph.

## Fact file

**Lives:** Worldwide

**Habitat:** Tropics in winter; polar areas in summer

**Length:** 50 feet

**Weight:** 70,000 pounds

**Life span:** 90 years

**Diet:** Krill and small fish

# Narwhal

- A narwhal's spiral tusk is actually a tooth that grows out of its upper lip; it can be up to ten feet long.

- Only males have a long tusk—some have two—but female narwhals sometimes have a short tusk.

- The tusk may have evolved to crack breathing holes in ice that covered the ocean, but scientists believe that they are now used primarily for attracting mates.

## Fact file

**Lives:** Arctic Ocean

**Habitat:** Cold waters

**Length:** 20 feet, including tusk

**Weight:** 3,500 pounds

**Life span:** 50 years

**Diet:** Fish, squid, and crustaceans

The tusks always grow in a spiral to the left, never to the right.

Hundreds of years ago, Danish sailors sold narwhal tusks, claiming that they were unicorn horns.

The tusk has millions of sensory nerves in it. These nerves may enable the narwhal to detect the temperature and saltiness of the water.

Apart from the tusk, narwhals have no other large teeth. They suck down their food and swallow it whole.

# Orca

- Also known as killer whales, orcas are large relatives of dolphins.

- Despite their name, these ocean hunters rarely attack humans in the wild.

- Whale watchers can identify an individual orca from the unique shape of its dorsal (back) fin and the pattern on its back.

- An orca's brain is four times bigger than a human's.

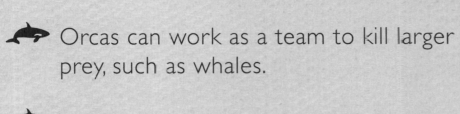 Orcas can work as a team to kill larger prey, such as whales.

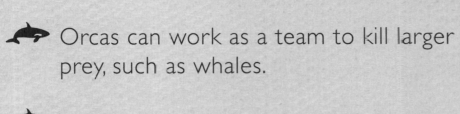 Orca mothers are pregnant for up to 18 months before their babies are born.

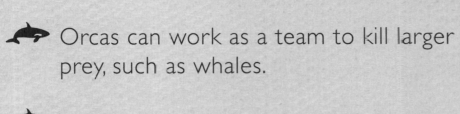 Orca pods specialize in hunting certain animals. Some attack seals, some eat fish, and others prey on whales.

## Fact file

**Lives:** Worldwide

**Habitat:** Colder waters

**Length:** 30 feet

**Weight:** 16,000 pounds

**Life span:** 50 years

**Diet:** Fish, squid, birds, seals, whales, and dolphins

# Bottlenose dolphin

🐬 A bottlenose dolphin has no nose—the pointed snout is actually its mouth.

🐬 When a dolphin is swimming fast, it jumps out of the water every now and then so it can take a breath.

🐬 The dolphin has up to 104 small teeth, which are used for grabbing slippery fish and shrimp.

🐬 Dolphins can leap up to 16 feet out of the water.

🐬 Dolphins make high-pitched squeaks that echo off of objects around them. The echoes help the dolphins find things in the water.

Dolphins will work together to herd a school of fish into a small area, making it easier for the dolphins to feed.

Dolphins have a poor sense of smell, but scientists believe they are able to detect different tastes.

## Fact file

**Lives:** Worldwide

**Habitat:** Deep and coastal waters

**Length:** 10 feet

**Weight:** 400 pounds

**Life span:** 45 years

**Diet:** Fish, cuttlefish, and crabs

# Manatee

- Manatees are also known as sea cows. Their closest living relative is the elephant.

- Manatees live in shallow water near the coast and often swim up rivers.

- Manatees look fat and blubbery, but most of their rounded bodies are filled up by a huge stomach.

- Lonely sailors mistook manatees for women swimming in the ocean. This is where the idea of mermaids comes from.

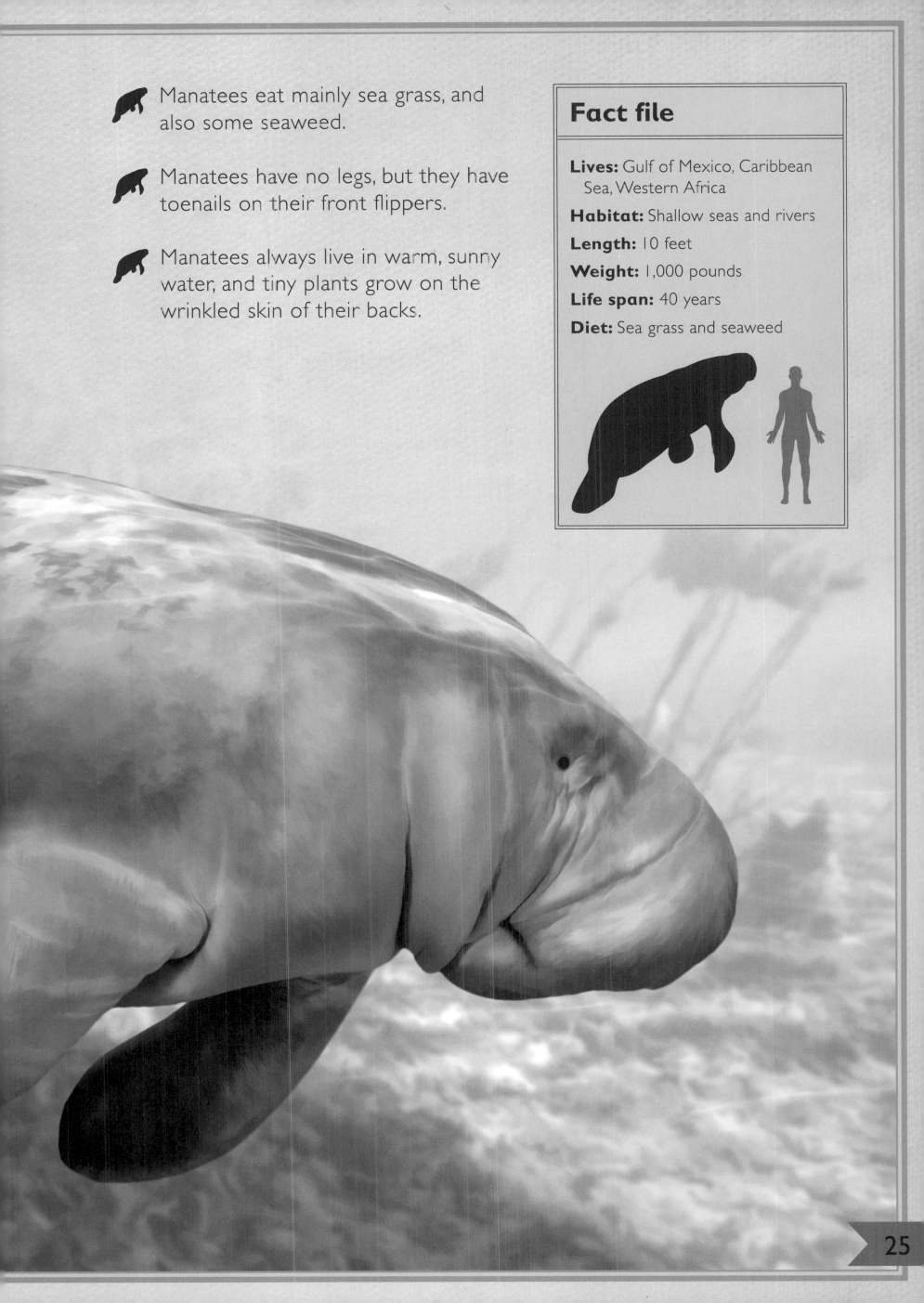

Manatees eat mainly sea grass, and also some seaweed.

Manatees have no legs, but they have toenails on their front flippers.

Manatees always live in warm, sunny water, and tiny plants grow on the wrinkled skin of their backs.

## Fact file

**Lives:** Gulf of Mexico, Caribbean Sea, Western Africa

**Habitat:** Shallow seas and rivers

**Length:** 10 feet

**Weight:** 1,000 pounds

**Life span:** 40 years

**Diet:** Sea grass and seaweed

# Yellowfin tuna

- This kind of tuna lives in large schools, often swimming alongside many different kinds of fish.

- The yellowfin is one of the world's fastest fish. It can swim at speeds up to 50 mph.

- The yellowfin can make its body warmer than the water around it.

- The fish pulls in the fins on its sides when it is swimming fast. This helps it to go even faster.

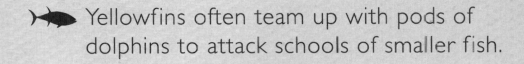 Yellowfins often team up with pods of dolphins to attack schools of smaller fish.

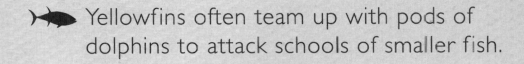 The yellowfin tuna gets its name from the color of the small fins that run along its body.

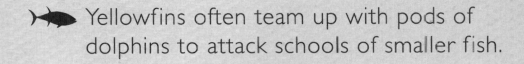 The long, curved fins near their tails keep these fish traveling straight in the water.

## Fact file

**Lives:** Worldwide

**Habitat:** Open ocean

**Length:** 7 feet

**Weight:** 400 pounds

**Life span:** 8 years

**Diet:** Fish and squid

# Marine iguana

- The marine iguana is the only lizard that gets all of its food from the ocean.

- The iguana dives down to the seabed to graze on seaweed at the bottom.

- Marine iguanas can dive about 35 feet and stay underwater for up to an hour, but they usually get out sooner because the water is too cold.

- The iguana's black skin helps to absorb sunlight so that it can warm up quickly.

- When there is little food available, the marine iguana actually shrinks itself a little so it doesn't need to eat as much.

## Fact file

**Lives:** Galápagos Islands

**Habitat:** Rocky coasts

**Length:** 4 feet

**Weight:** 25 pounds

**Life span:** 10 years

**Diet:** Seaweed and algae

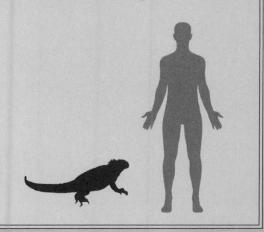

During the breeding season, chemicals in the seaweed the iguana eats make a male's skin brightly colored, helping it to attract a mate.

The crest of spines along its back helps the lizard to swim straight underwater.

# Whale shark

- This shark is the largest saltwater fish in the world.

- Despite being a shark, this fish does not hunt. Instead it eats plankton and other tiny animals.

- A whale shark never stops swimming. To eat, it keeps its mouth open and filters out food from the water using its gills.

- The whale shark has about 3,000 small teeth.

## Fact file

**Lives:** Worldwide

**Habitat:** Warm oceans

**Length:** 30 feet

**Weight:** 40,000 pounds

**Life span:** 70 years

**Diet:** Plankton and fish

Every whale shark has a unique pattern of blotches on its back.

Approximately 25 gallons of water passes through a whale shark's mouth every minute.

Although they are big, whale sharks are slow swimmers. They swim only about three miles per hour.

# Great white shark

- The great white is the largest hunting fish in the world.

- It has a supersensitive nose that can smell blood in the water miles away.

- A great white attacks from behind. Just before it bites, it shuts its eyes so they don't get damaged during the impact.

- Great whites take a small bite of their victim first, in order to weaken them.

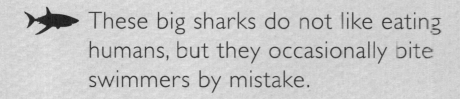 These big sharks do not like eating humans, but they occasionally bite swimmers by mistake.

The shark's skin is covered in tiny, hooked scales. These help its body to cut through water as it swims.

A shark's snout can detect the electricity produced by living bodies. It uses this sense to find prey in dark water.

## Fact file

**Lives:** Worldwide

**Habitat:** Oceans

**Length:** 18 feet

**Weight:** 5,000 pounds

**Life span:** 70 years

**Diet:** Fish, seals, birds, and small whales

# Ocean sunfish

The sunfish is the largest bony fish in the world. Only sharks, which have skeletons made of cartilage rather than bone, are bigger.

This fish gets its name from the way it basks in the sunshine at the surface.

The sunfish is as tall as it is long.

The sunfish cannot close its mouth, which is lined with a ridge of teeth used for bursting jellyfish.

The sunfish's slimy skin gets covered with tiny parasites. Smaller fish and birds eat these parasites, and the sunfish can also leap out of the water to knock them off when they hit the water.

A female sunfish produces more than 300 million eggs every year.

Baby sunfish have to grow 60 million times larger to become adults.

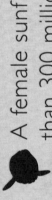

# Manta ray

- The manta ray's smooth skin is covered in slime to prevent germs from growing on it.

- Rays are related to sharks.

- Rays swim by flapping their wide fins up and down like wings.

- The ray curves the flaps near its mouth into a funnel to help it filter food from the water.

- This giant fish does slow somersaults through clouds of plankton as it feeds.

The female manta ray does not lay eggs; it usually gives birth to a single baby every few years. Sometimes rays give birth to two babies at a time.

Manta rays visit "cleaning stations" at coral reefs, where smaller fish nibble their skin clean.

## Fact file

**Lives:** Worldwide

**Habitat:** Warm oceans

**Length:** 20 feet

**Weight:** 2,500 pounds

**Life span:** 50 years

**Diet:** Plankton

# Oarfish

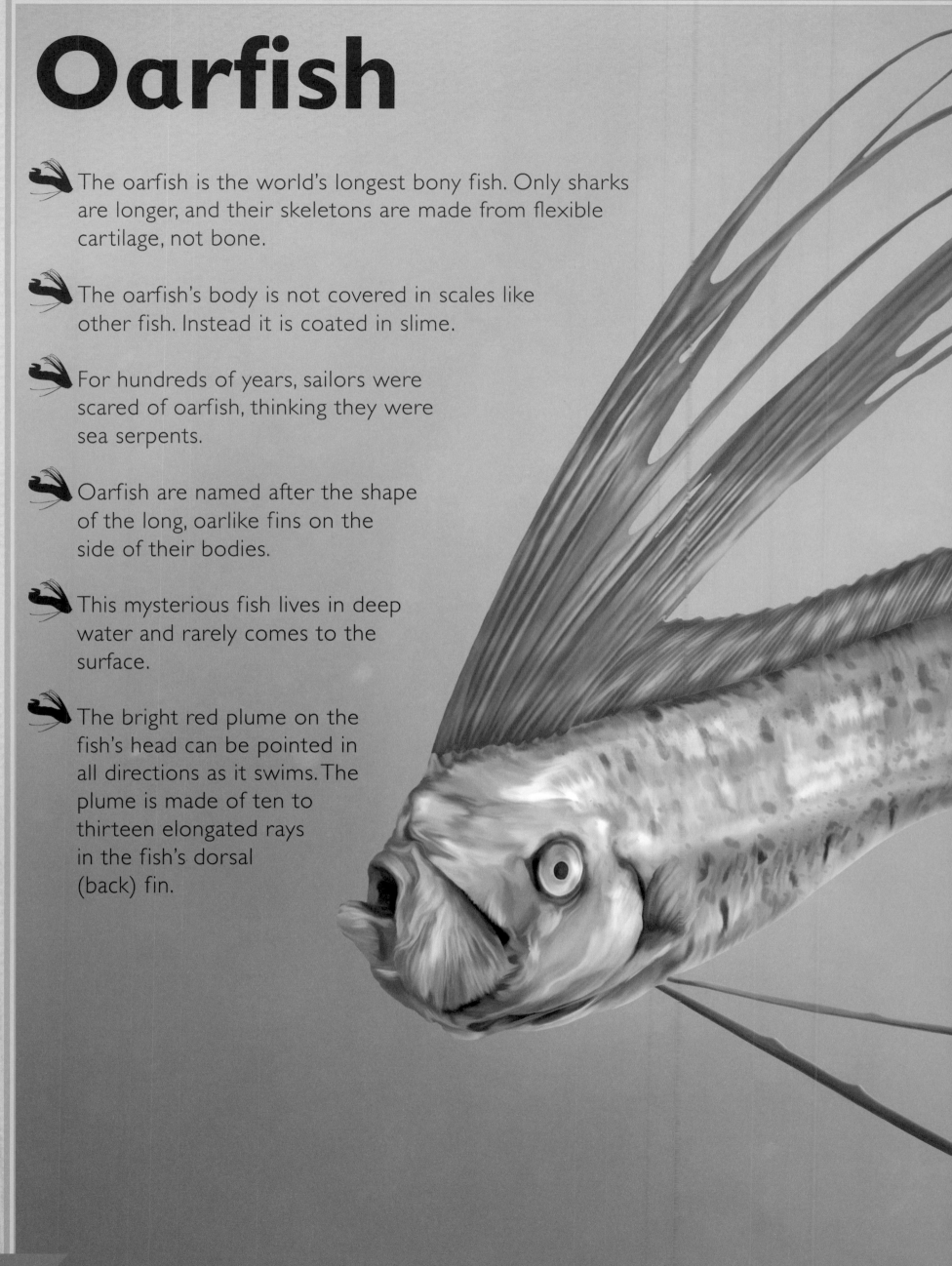

- The oarfish is the world's longest bony fish. Only sharks are longer, and their skeletons are made from flexible cartilage, not bone.

- The oarfish's body is not covered in scales like other fish. Instead it is coated in slime.

- For hundreds of years, sailors were scared of oarfish, thinking they were sea serpents.

- Oarfish are named after the shape of the long, oarlike fins on the side of their bodies.

- This mysterious fish lives in deep water and rarely comes to the surface.

- The bright red plume on the fish's head can be pointed in all directions as it swims. The plume is made of ten to thirteen elongated rays in the fish's dorsal (back) fin.

## Fact file

**Lives:** Worldwide

**Habitat:** Warm oceans

**Length:** 36 feet

**Weight:** 600 pounds

**Life span:** Unknown

**Diet:** Krill and plankton

# Humpback anglerfish

🐟 The anglerfish has a glowing "fishing rod" on its head to attract smaller fish—which it then gobbles up.

🐟 The glowing lure produces light using chemicals, but it does not get hot like a lightbulb.

🐟 Anglerfish live in deep, dark water where the only light comes from their "fishing rods."

🐟 All large anglerfish are female. The males are tiny creatures that fuse to the female in order to mate. After mating, the male lets go.

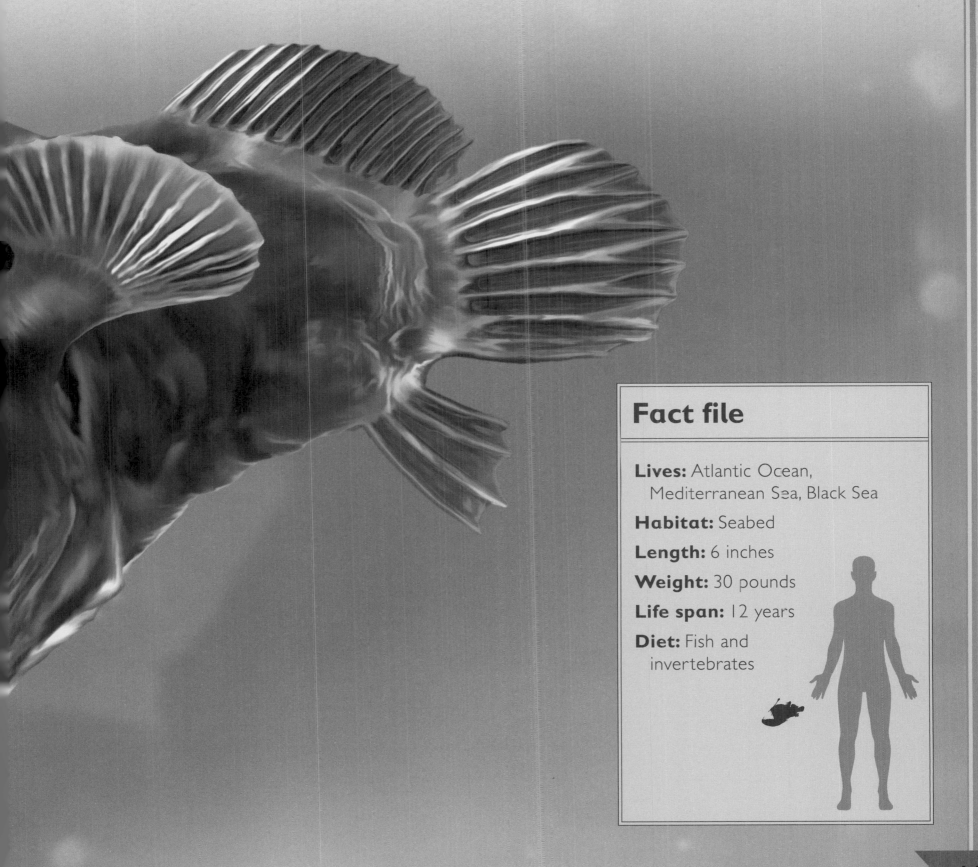

- Anglerfish are also called monkfish, sea toads, and batfish.

- The anglerfish's sharp teeth are transparent.

- The anglerfish's huge mouth is almost as wide as its body is long.

## Fact file

**Lives:** Atlantic Ocean, Mediterranean Sea, Black Sea

**Habitat:** Seabed

**Length:** 6 inches

**Weight:** 30 pounds

**Life span:** 12 years

**Diet:** Fish and invertebrates

# Seahorse

- Seahorses cannot swim very well. They wrap their tails around seaweed so they don't float away.

- A seahorse uses its tube-shaped mouth to suck in tiny shrimp that float in the water.

- The male seahorses carry eggs inside a pouch, and are one of the few male animals to give birth.

- The seahorse can flap its tiny fins 35 times a second.

- Seahorses can move their eyes independently so that they can look forward and backward at the same time.

- Seahorses change their color to match the seaweed around them.

- A baby seahorse may eat up to 3,000 shrimp every day.

## Fact file

**Lives:** Eastern Atlantic Ocean and Mediterranean Sea

**Habitat:** Seaweeds

**Length:** 1–14 inches

**Weight:** 1–16 ounces

**Life span:** 3 years

**Diet:** Shrimp and plankton

# Queen parrotfish

- The queen parrotfish's teeth are fused together to make a beak. This is a defining feature of all parrotfish species.

- Parrotfish scrape tiny bits of seaweed and coral off the rocky seabed.

- They swallow chunks of coral and then pass them out as sand.

- Parrotfish are all born female. As they age, hormones kick in and transform them into males. They can breed during both stages of life, laying eggs while female and fertilizing the eggs of others while male.

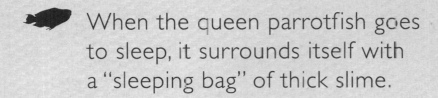 When the queen parrotfish goes to sleep, it surrounds itself with a "sleeping bag" of thick slime.

Scientists believe that the slimy bubble around the fish helps to keep its smell from spreading through the water, so that hunters cannot find it.

The flesh of some parrotfish species contains a poison that causes breathing problems in humans who eat the animals.

## Fact file

**Lives:** Western Atlantic Ocean

**Habitat:** Coral reefs

**Length:** 6–10 inches

**Weight:** 22 pounds

**Life span:** 7 years

**Diet:** Algae and dead coral

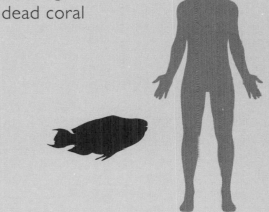

# Clownfish

- This colorful fish makes its home among the tentacles of a sea anemone (a marine animal that looks like a flower).

- The anemone's tentacles are covered in stingers, but the clownfish's skin contains a slimy mucus that protects it from the anemone's stings.

- The clownfish does not swim far from its home. If danger appears, it races back to the safety of the anemone.

- In return for its protection, the fish cleans away any dirt that builds up in the anemone.

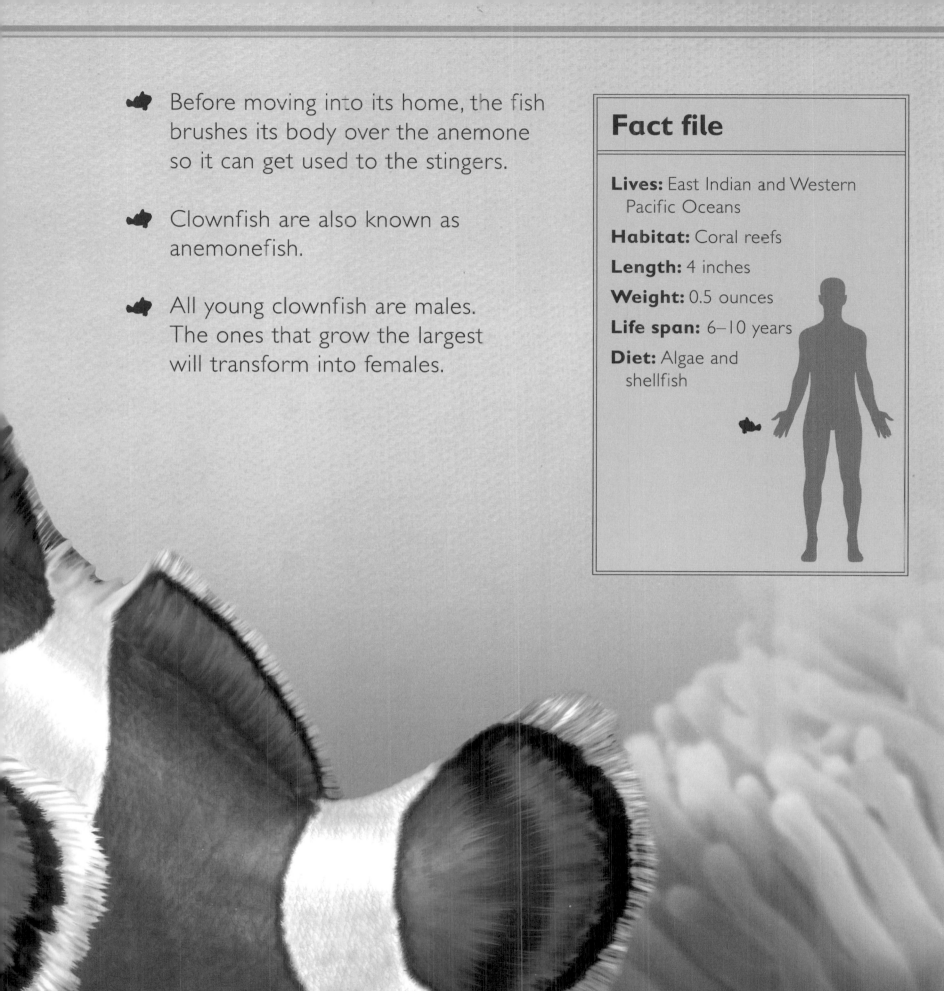

- Before moving into its home, the fish brushes its body over the anemone so it can get used to the stingers.

- Clownfish are also known as anemonefish.

- All young clownfish are males. The ones that grow the largest will transform into females.

## Fact file

**Lives:** East Indian and Western Pacific Oceans

**Habitat:** Coral reefs

**Length:** 4 inches

**Weight:** 0.5 ounces

**Life span:** 6–10 years

**Diet:** Algae and shellfish

# Green sea turtle

- Male sea turtles rarely come onto land—but the females will come out of the water to lay eggs on a beach.

- Unlike land tortoises, sea turtles cannot pull their heads into their shells.

- Females usually lay their eggs at night.

- Adult females lay their eggs on the same beach that they themselves hatched on.

- Green sea turtles float at the surface on sunny days to warm up in the sunshine.

Sea turtles can sleep on the seabed, holding their breath for several hours.

When swimming fast, the turtle must come to the surface every few minutes to breathe.

## Fact file

**Lives:** Worldwide

**Habitat:** Warm oceans

**Length:** 5 feet

**Weight:** 700 pounds

**Life span:** 100 years

**Diet:** Seaweed anc jellyfish

# Lionfish

- The lionfish is also called the turkeyfish because its long, spiked fins look like the bird's feathers.

- The hollow spines on the back of the lionfish are covered in a poisonous slime that protects it from predators.

- The fish uses camouflage and speed to capture its prey, usually smaller fish and shrimp.

- A lionfish sting hurts but does not usually kill humans. Soaking the area in hot water will reduce the effects of the poison.

- When threatened, the lionfish swims with its head down so its poisonous spines face its attacker.

- Its large fins and spines warn predators to stay away.

- Lionfish are cannibals and will eat each other if there is no other food around.

## Fact file

**Lives:** Indian and Western Pacific Oceans

**Habitat:** Rocky reefs

**Length:** 12–15 inches

**Weight:** 2 pounds

**Life span:** 10 years

**Diet:** Fish and shrimp

# Sailfish

- The sailfish is one of the fastest fish in the world. It can swim at speeds up to 68 mph.

- The "sail" is the tall fin that runs along the fish's back.

- The fish raises and lowers this tall fin to scare away attackers and to herd schools of fish.

- Sailfish catch their prey by working together to gather schools of smaller fish into a tight space and then darting in to take a bite.

Sailfish belong to a group called "billfish," which includes swordfish, spearfish, and marlin. All these species have long, pointed snouts, or bills.

These fish can change the color of the stripes along their bodies. They do this to send signals to other sailfish.

## Fact file

**Lives:** Worldwide

**Habitat:** Warm oceans

**Length:** 6–11 feet

**Weight:** 120–220 pounds

**Life span:** 4 years

**Diet:** Fish

# Flying fish

- Flying fish do not really fly. They leap out of the water at high speeds and then glide on their winglike fins.

- The fish glide to escape from larger predators that are attacking them underwater.

- There are 40 types of flying fish; most of them can glide for up to 160 feet.

- The longest recorded "flight" of a flying fish saw the fish stay in the air for 45 seconds.

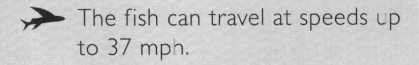 The fish can travel at speeds up to 37 mph.

When it returns to the surface of the water, the fish can flap its tail fins and propel itself back into the air.

If they catch the wind, flying fish can leap high enough to glide over a boat.

## Fact file

**Lives:** Worldwide

**Habitat:** Warm oceans

**Length:** 10–18 inches

**Weight:** 1 pound

**Life span:** 5 years

**Diet:** Plankton

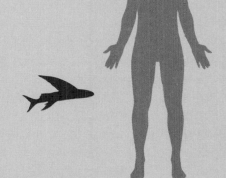

# Tufted puffin

- The tufted puffin swims underwater to catch fish, using its wings as flippers to push through the water.

- The puffin can catch several fish in one dive and can hold a dozen fish sideways in its beak.

- Puffins have been observed carrying more than 60 fish in their mouth at one time.

The puffin uses its beak and feet to dig a nest into a grassy slope or muddy cliff.

A pair of tufted puffins usually has one chick every year. Both the male and female bring the chick fish from the ocean to eat.

The tufted puffin is the largest type of puffin. It is named for the tufts of yellow feathers on its head.

In winter, puffins leave their nests and go hunting far out at sea.

## Fact file

**Lives:** North Pacific Ocean

**Habitat:** Coastal waters

**Length:** 15 inches

**Weight:** 1.6 pounds

**Life span:** 20 years

**Diet:** Fish

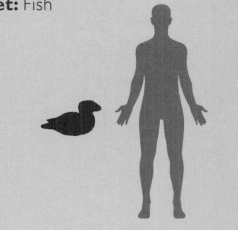

# Emperor penguin

- The emperor penguin is the largest of the 17 types of penguin.

- The penguins can withstand some of the most extreme weather on Earth. In the winter, the Antarctic air can reach -76°F, and the winds blow at hurricane strength.

- Only the male penguins spend the winter on land. They stay there to look after their eggs.

- Penguins balance their egg—and the chick once it hatches—on their feet and keep it warm inside a pouch in their stomach feathers.

- When the chick hatches, its father feeds it with a milky liquid from its stomach until the mother returns.

When spring arrives, the females walk about 50 miles over the ice to take over the responsibility of caring for the young chicks from their mates.

## Fact file

**Lives:** Southern Ocean

**Habitat:** Cold water, Antarctica

**Length:** 3–4 feet

**Weight:** 80 pounds

**Life span:** 20 years

**Diet:** Fish and squid

# Pelican

- Pelicans have the longest beaks of any bird. Some grow to 16 inches.

- The pelican's beak holds a large bag of skin, which is used for scooping fish out of the water.

- The bird scoops up a beakful of water and then squirts it out, leaving any fish trapped inside.

- Young pelicans feed by taking food out of their parents' beaks.

## Fact file

**Lives:** Worldwide

**Habitat:** Coastlines

**Length:** 4–6 feet

**Weight:** 6–30 pounds

**Life span:** 25 years

**Diet:** Fish

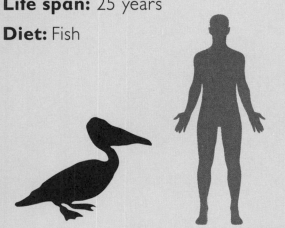

Pelicans' nostrils are nearly closed, so they have to open their mouths to breathe in.

The pelican is one of the heaviest flying birds in the world—especially when it is flapping along with a beakful of fish.

A pelican's bones contain large pockets of air, which helps it to stay afloat in water.

# Giant clam

- A giant clam sucks in seawater to filter out tiny bits of food floating in it.

- The clam's bright colors come from microscopic plants, called algae, growing inside its body.

- The clam protects the algae, and in return the algae supplies the clam with sugar.

- Tiny transparent pea crabs live inside the clam's body, feeding off of its food supply.

- The clam cannot swim away from attackers. Fish and other predators can nibble on the clam whenever they want.

- Some stories suggest that divers can get their arms trapped inside a giant clam, but this is a myth. The clam cannot shut its shell completely.

- Millions of baby giant clams are released into the water each year, but only one or two will grow to full size.

## Fact file

**Lives:** Indian and Pacific Oceans
**Habitat:** Coral reefs
**Length:** 4 feet
**Weight:** 440 pounds
**Life span:** 100 years
**Diet:** Plankton

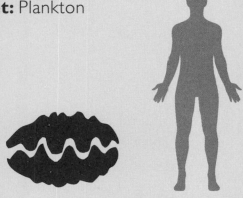

# Lobster

- A lobster is blue when it is alive. It turns red only after it has been cooked.

- When they migrate, lobsters form single-file lines. When resting or threatened, they form a circle with their antennae facing outward to deter predators.

- Baby lobsters are about an inch long. They swim in the water for a while and then hide in crevices.

- A female lobster carries her bright red eggs under her tail for about ten weeks.

An adult lobster sheds its hard shell once a year. ts body is very soft for several days afterward.

If a lobster loses a leg, it can grow another one

Lobsters communicate with each other by pumping smelly urine into each other's faces.

## Fact file

**Lives:** Worldwide

**Habitat:** Rocky and sandy seabeds

**Length:** 1–3 feet

**Weight:** 4–20 pounds

**Life span:** 50 years

**Diet:** Crustaceans, fish, and mollusks

# Giant Pacific octopus

- The giant Pacific octopus is the largest octopus species in the world. Its arms can spread up to 20 feet from one tip to another.

- The only hard body part is the hooked beak at the base of the eight long arms.

- An octopus can squeeze through any space it can fit its beak into, so this giant can pass through a hole the size of a lemon.

- The octopus can change color to match the seabed—and even make its skin texture rough like the rocks.

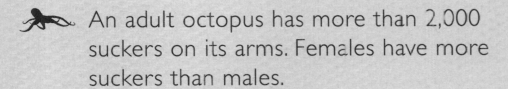 An adult octopus has more than 2,000 suckers on its arms. Females have more suckers than males.

A female octopus lays up to 100,000 eggs in a cave and spends about six months inside the cave pumping clean water over them.

The mother octopus starves as she cares for her eggs, and dies soon after the babies hatch.

## Fact file

**Lives:** North Pacific Ocean

**Habitat:** Seabed

**Length:** 10–20 feet

**Weight:** 20–100 pounds

**Life span:** 4 years

**Diet:** Fish, shrimp, sharks, and birds

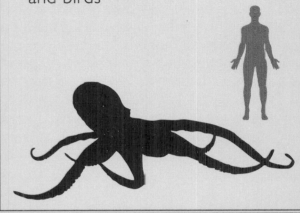

# Giant squid

- The giant squid is the largest animal in the world that does not have a backbone.

- When giant squid need to move fast, they squirt water out from their bodies to move at more than 25 mph over short distances.

- Giant squid are thought to use their two long tentacles to catch prey. They glow in the dark water and attract fish.

- The suckers on the squid have a ring of teeth around them that cut into prey.

- When giant squid are attacked by sperm whales, they use their hooked beaks to fight back.

- A giant squid's eyes are as big as a human head!

## Fact file

**Lives:** Worldwide

**Habitat:** Deep ocean waters

**Length:** 20–30 feet

**Weight:** 300–600 pounds

**Life span:** 5 years

**Diet:** Fish, shrimp, and other squid

# Insulamon freshwater crab

- This brightly colored crab lives on only a few islands in the Indian Ocean.

- Crabs grow by molting—they grow a new shell under the old one, which they break out of and leave behind.

- The crab has a tail, but it is folded under its body all the time.

- This species of crab lives exclusively in freshwater.

The insulamon's purple color allows it to spot a mate of its own species and not get confused by other kinds of crabs.

The largest male insulamon crabs are red, not purple, though. The red color may be a sign of their strength.

You can tell male and female crabs apart by the shape of their tail. Males have a triangular and pointed tail, whi e females have a broader, rounder one.

## Fact file

**Lives:** Philippines

**Habitat:** Rivers and shoreline

**Length:** 2 inches

**Weight:** 3.5 ounces

**Life span:** 2 years

**Diet:** Fish and invertebrates

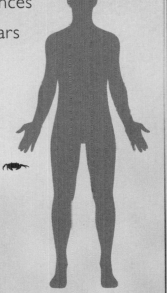

# Sea slug

- Sea slugs are distant relatives of land slugs and snails, but they don't have an external shell.

- Sea slugs are brightly colored to warn predators that their bodies are filled with poisonous chemicals.

- Some sea slugs collect the stingers from the jellyfish they eat and place them in their skin to fend off attackers.

- Sea slugs are male and female at the same time, but they cannot produce babies by themselves.

- Sea slugs breathe in water with feathery gills that poke out of their backs.

## Fact file

**Lives:** Indian and Pacific Oceans

**Habitat:** Seabed

**Length:** 0.25–12 inches

**Weight:** 0.3–3.3 pounds

**Life span:** 1 year

**Diet:** Algae, coral, barnacles, sponges, jellyfish, and anemones

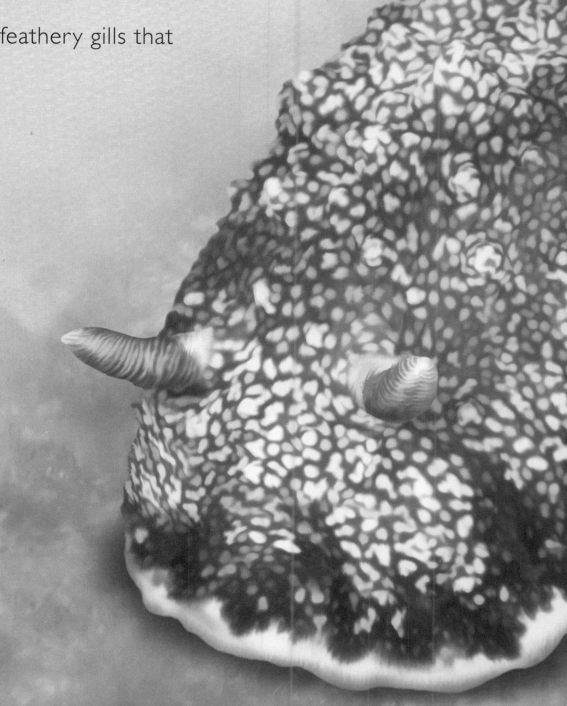

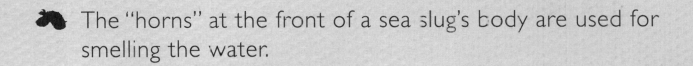 The "horns" at the front of a sea slug's body are used for smelling the water.

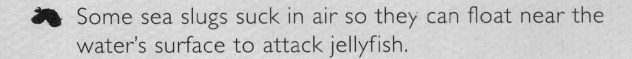 Some sea slugs suck in air so they can float near the water's surface to attack jellyfish.

# Sea star

* Most but not all sea stars have five limbs. The sunflower sea star has between 16 and 24 limbs, and other species can have up to 50 limbs.

* Sea stars move by pumping water around tubes in their bodies.

* Sea stars are often called starfish, but they are not fish. They are relatives of sea urchins and sea cucumbers.

* If a predator bites off a sea star's limb, it will grow a new one, but this takes about a year.

* Sea stars do not have a shell, but they have hard bony plates under their skin.

* A sea star's mouth is on the underside of its body. Its anus is on the top of its body.

* Sea stars see with their arms. They have about 100 tiny eyes all over the tips.

## Fact file

**Lives:** Worldwide
**Habitat:** Seabed
**Length:** 4–9 inches
**Weight:** 5–10 ounces
**Life span:** 35 years
**Diet:** Shellfish

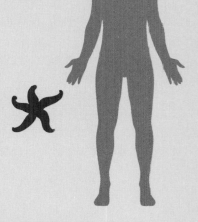

# Lion's mane jellyfish

- This jellyfish is the largest in the world. It can have more than 800 tentacles hanging from its bell-shaped body.

- The jellyfish's tentacles can trail 120 feet into the water—which is longer than a blue whale.

- Their tentacles are covered in tiny stingers that inject poison into anything they touch. A sting is painful to humans, but rarely causes death.

- Once fish and other prey have been caught, they are slowly pulled up the tentacles to the jellyfish's mouth.

- A jellyfish has only one opening on its body. Food goes in through the same space that waste comes out of.

- Baby jellyfish stay stuck to rocks with their tentacles pointing upward. They swim off when they get big enough.

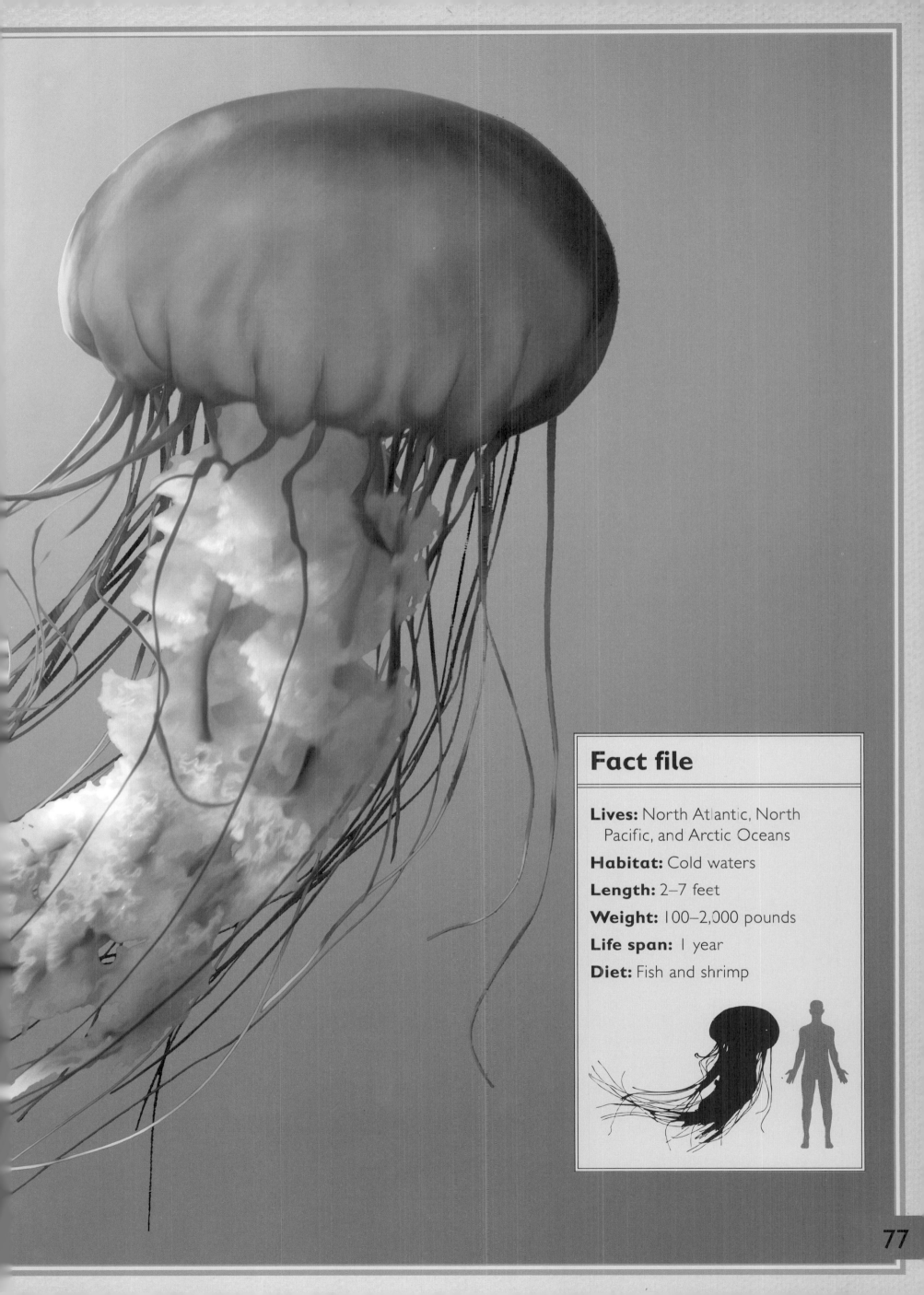

## Fact file

**Lives:** North Atlantic, North Pacific, and Arctic Oceans

**Habitat:** Cold waters

**Length:** 2–7 feet

**Weight:** 100–2,000 pounds

**Life span:** 1 year

**Diet:** Fish and shrimp

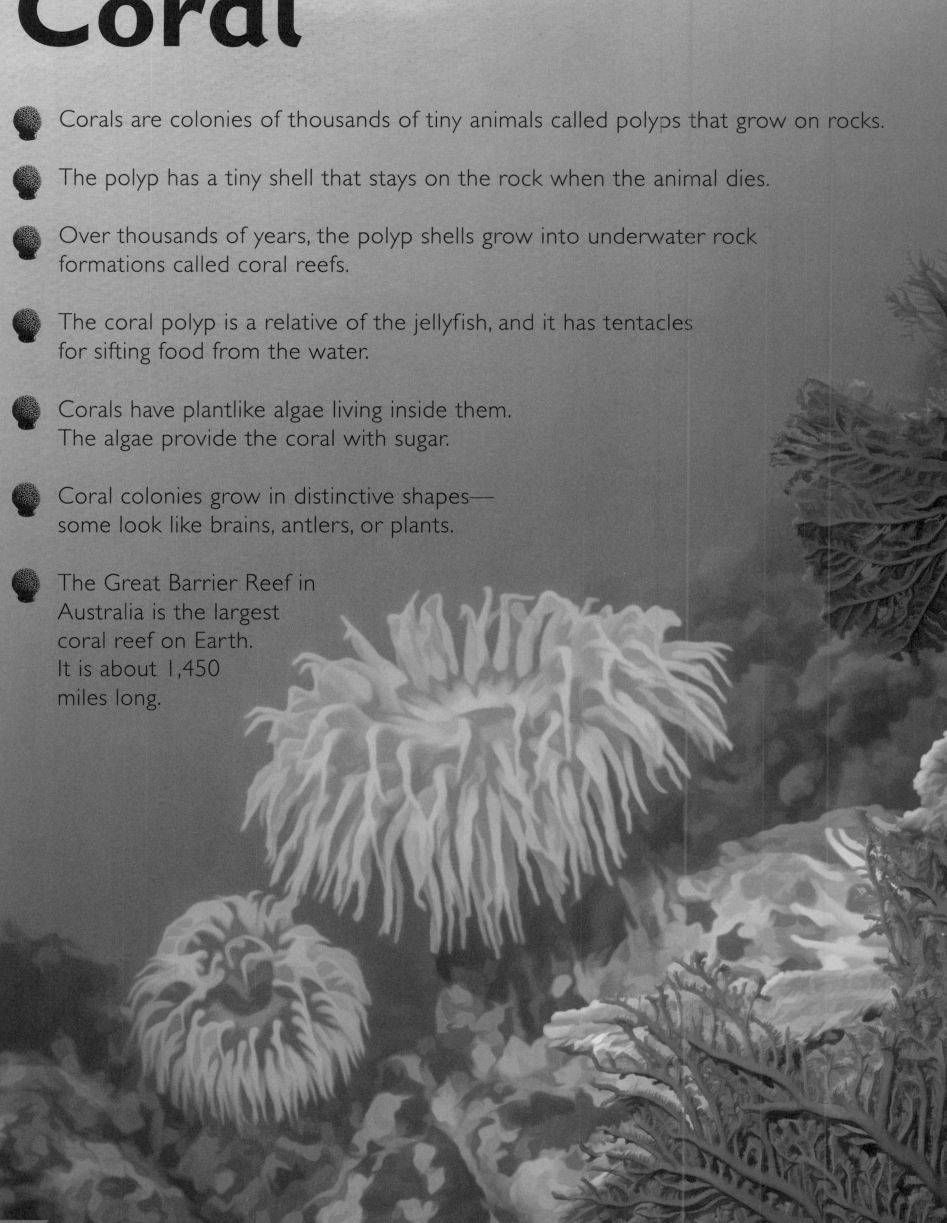

# Coral

- Corals are colonies of thousands of tiny animals called polyps that grow on rocks.

- The polyp has a tiny shell that stays on the rock when the animal dies.

- Over thousands of years, the polyp shells grow into underwater rock formations called coral reefs.

- The coral polyp is a relative of the jellyfish, and it has tentacles for sifting food from the water.

- Corals have plantlike algae living inside them. The algae provide the coral with sugar.

- Coral colonies grow in distinctive shapes— some look like brains, antlers, or plants.

- The Great Barrier Reef in Australia is the largest coral reef on Earth. It is about 1,450 miles long.

## Fact file

**Brain coral**

**Lives:** Worldwide

**Habitat:** Warm, shallow seas

**Length:** 6 feet

**Life span:** Hundreds of years

**Diet:** Plankton

# Ocean World

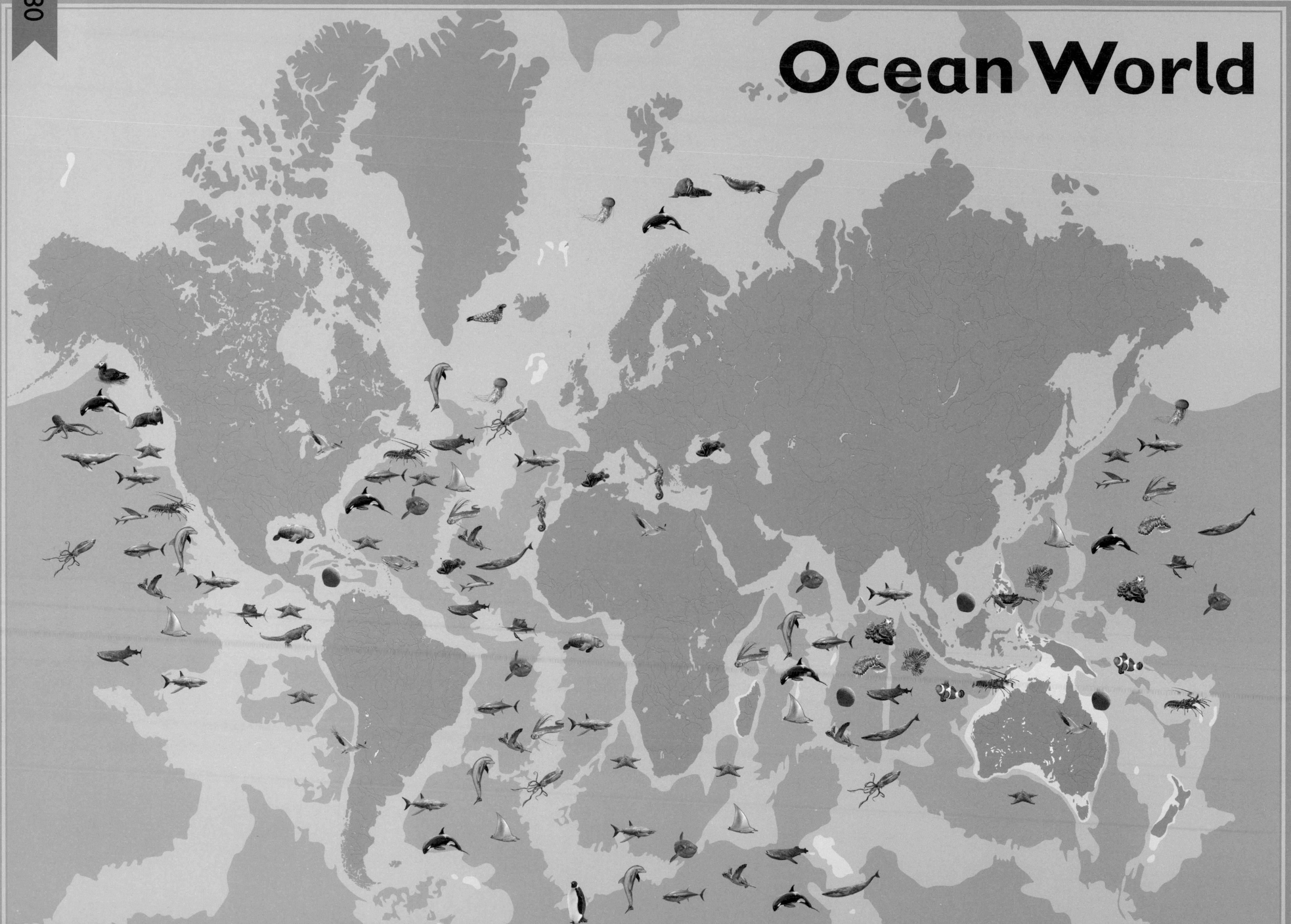